W9-CJM-430

3 1526 05178778 3

KIDS' DAY OUT

Museums

Joanne Mattern

RED
CHAIR
·PRESS·

Kids' Day Out is produced and published by Red Chair Press:

Red Chair Press LLC   PO Box 333   South Egremont, MA 01258-0333

www.redchairpress.com

Publisher's Cataloging-In-Publication Data

Names: Mattern, Joanne, 1963–

Title: Museums / Joanne Mattern.

Description: Egremont, MA : Red Chair Press, [2018] | Series: Kids' day out | Interest age level: 007-010. | Includes index and glossary. | Summary: "Do you like to collect things? Many people do. Some people collect art. Others collect objects from history. Some people collect cars or toys. You can collect just about anything! There are almost as many museums as there are things to collect. Take a trip back in time and learn more about these amazing places."-- Provided by publisher.

Identifiers: ISBN 978-1-63440-390-0 (library hardcover) | ISBN 978-1-63440-394-8 (ebook)

Subjects: LCSH: Museums--History--Juvenile literature. | CYAC: Museums--History.

Classification: LCC AM5 .M38 2018 (print) | LCC AM5 (ebook) | DDC 069.09--dc23

Copyright © 2019 Red Chair Press LLC
RED CHAIR PRESS, the RED CHAIR and associated logos are registered trademarks of Red Chair Press LLC.

All rights reserved. No part of this book may be reproduced, stored in an information or retrieval system, or transmitted in any form by any means, electronic, mechanical including photocopying, recording, or otherwise without the prior written permission from the Publisher. For permissions, contact info@redchairpress.com

Photo credits: p. 1, 3, 4, 5, 6, 7, 8, 9, 10, 11, 12, 15, 16: iStock; Cover, p. 18, 19, 22, 24, 25, 26, 28, 29, 30: Dreamstime; p. Cover, 14, 15, 17, 27, 31: Alamy; p. 28, 30: Ingimage; p. 20: National Park Service; p. 21: Greg Pease, courtesy of Friends of Fort McHenry

Printed in the United States of America

0518 1P CGBF18

Contents

Amazing Collections

Do you like to collect things? Many people do. Some people collect art. Others collect objects from history. Some people collect cars or toys. You can collect just about anything!

A museum is a place that holds a collection of objects. These objects are important in some way. They might be links to history. They might be paintings. Or they might be something unusual, like a type of clothing.

There are almost as many museums as there are things to collect. Museums can teach us many things. Let's take a trip back in time and find out more about these amazing places.

It's a Fact

There are more than 55,000 museums in 202 countries.

Ancient Collectors

People have been collecting objects that interested them since the beginning of time. Archaeologists, or scientists who study the past, have found collections of objects in burial sites that are thousands of years old. Ancient cave paintings show that early humans valued art and used it as a way to tell stories.

Even though early people collected objects that were important to them, these collections were not museums. However, they show that people like to keep important objects. These objects also tell us about life in ancient times.

Scientists learn about how people lived when they study items like these arrowheads and Roman urns.

The Parthenon was a temple in Athens more than 2,200 years ago.

Emperors and other rich people in ancient Greece and Rome kept collections of valuable objects. Archaeologists discovered a room filled with paintings honoring the gods in an ancient Greek building called the Parthenon. Roman emperors also collected art and statues. However, these collections were only for the emperors and their family and friends. Ordinary people never got to see them.

Chinese emperors also liked to collect things. Emperor Wu-ti, who ruled from 141 to 86 B.C., collected paintings from different parts of China. In the Middle East and Africa, many people collected and displayed religious objects.

It's a Fact

Some ancient collections were displayed in "wonder rooms."

Royal Collections

Between the 12th and 16th centuries in Europe, royal families also collected objects. As trade developed between countries, kings and princes were able to collect objects from other parts of Europe.

Many of the royal collections were kept in palaces and ordinary people never got to see them. However, other collectors had a different idea. The Capitoline Museum is located in Italy. It is the oldest collection of public art in the world. The Museum was started in 1471 when Pope Sixtus IV donated a group of ancient sculptures to the people of Rome. Another pope, Pope Julius II, also displayed sculptures in his Vatican Museum.

The Capitoline Museum in the center of Rome

It's a Fact

While many royal collections included art, others included historical objects and scientific objects.

The Ashmolean museum in Oxford, England

The First Museums

As time passed, ideas about collecting began to change. Instead of just collecting objects they liked, people began to collect objects that had meaning or that were related to each other. They also wanted a way to keep their collections together as time passed. Many of these people started museums. These museums were a way to keep collections together and make them available to the public.

In England, a man named Elias Ashmole collected a huge amount of paintings and objects. After a while, he had no place to keep his collections. In 1660, he offered them to Oxford University. The university built a special building to hold the collection. The Ashmolean Museum opened in 1683. It was the first museum that was open to the public.

It's a Fact

The Ashmolean displayed the stuffed body of an extinct bird called the dodo.

In 1759, the British Museum opened in London. The museum started because the government felt a responsibility to preserve collections "for the general use and benefit of the public." The first collections in the British Museum were manuscripts, art, coins, and scientific and natural objects.

It's a Fact

When the British Museum first opened, officials thought large crowds would damage the artifacts. Visitors had to apply in writing for admission tickets.

Meanwhile, people in France were unhappy that they could not see royal art collections. In 1793, the Louvre art museum opened in Paris. Today, the Louvre is the most visited museum in the world. More than eight million people visit every year.

In 1819, the Museo del Prado opened in Madrid. The museum had originally been built in 1785 to house a collection of natural history items. By 1819, it had changed into a place to exhibit art.

Madrid's Museo del Prado

The Louvre in Paris

America's First Museums

American Philosophical Society, Philadelphia, PA

It's a Fact

Benjamin Franklin was a member of the American Philosophical Society and helped start their museum.

Museums began to appear in the United States during the 1700s and 1800s as well. The oldest museum in the United States was started by the American Philosophical Society in Philadelphia. It opened in 1743. The museum displayed objects about American history and science.

In 1773, the Charleston Library Society in South Carolina opened the Charleston Museum. Its purpose was to promote agriculture and herbal medicine. Charleston was a private museum at first. It opened to the public in 1824.

Many museums opened during the late 1800s and early 1900s. Some of these museums focused on natural history. The American Museum of Natural History started in a building in New York City's Central Park. In 1874, construction started on a new building. The museum opened in 1877. Today, it is one of the largest museums in the world.

Large art museums were also built in American cities during this time. The Metropolitan Museum of Art opened in New York City in 1872. The Art Institute of Chicago opened in 1883. Today, these museums are some of the most popular art museums in the world.

It's a Fact

The Metropolitan Museum of Art is the largest art museum in the United States. It is also the most popular, with more than six million visitors every year.

Something for Everyone

While you might think of an art museum or a natural history museum, these are not the only kinds of museums. There is a museum for just about every interest.

Some museums are dedicated to a single person or family. Many times, these museums are located in the home where the person lived. President Franklin D. Roosevelt lived in Hyde Park, New York, and his home is now a museum about his life. There are also museums for writers, artists, and other important public figures.

It's a Fact

Living history museums don't just display objects. People dressed in costume act out events to bring the time period to life for visitors.

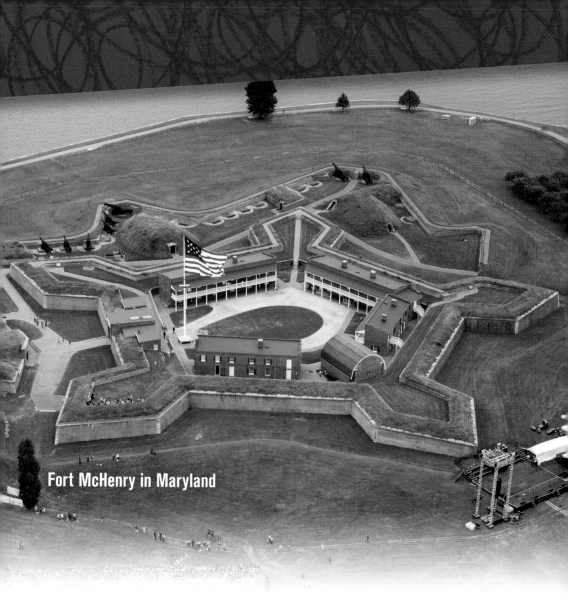
Fort McHenry in Maryland

Other museums focus on a historical time period or event. The Museum of the American Revolution in Philadelphia tells the story of America's fight for freedom. Visitors to Fort McHenry can view exhibits and buildings from the War of 1812.

Antique cars in a museum in Ankara, Turkey

Some museums have exhibits about a lot of different things. Others focus on just a few. There are museums that feature old cars or old toys. There are museums dedicated to quilts, shells, beads, and teeth. California has a museum about bananas. Hawaii has a museum about teddy bears. Every sport has a museum that focuses on great players and achievements.

Many people visit wax museums and oddity museums. The most famous wax museum is Madame Tussaud's in London. Madame Tussaud's features wax figures of famous people. Oddity museums such as Ripley's Believe it Or Not also feature wax figures and objects that focus on the weirdest parts of life.

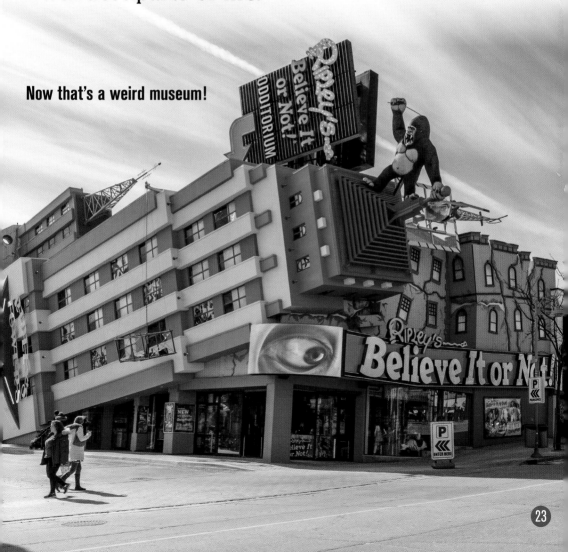

Now that's a weird museum!

Please Touch!

Many museums do not let visitors get too close to the exhibit. Paintings might be roped off. Objects might be in glass cases. Visitors are warned not to touch anything. While these rules are important to protect the objects, they can make museums less fun than they should be.

In the past few years, many museums have allowed visitors to touch and take part in the exhibits. Many science museums feature exhibits for visitors to play with. There is always a lot to do at a science museum like Liberty Science Center in New Jersey. Here visitors can crawl through exhibits and work with machines.

Children's Museum, Brooklyn, NY

It's a Fact

Even museums that don't allow visitors to touch the exhibits often have a play or creative fun area for children to enjoy.

Children's museums are also fun places to play. These museums provide games and toys for young children. Visitors can paint, make music, dress in costume, or play with Legos or other toys.

Behind the Scenes

Many people work or volunteer in museums. Some are tour guides. They lead visitors around the museum and explain the different exhibits. Others prepare the exhibits. They do research, collect objects, and display them for visitors to see. Still more people work behind the scenes. They might run the museum's web site or print visitor guides.

People who take care of museum collections are called curators. Many curators go to college to learn how to take care of their collections. It is important to know how to find great exhibits and how to put them on display.

Museums Forever!

Millions of people visit museums in the United States every year. Millions more visit museums in other parts of the world. More people go to museums than go to sporting events or concerts.

There is something for everyone at museums. Whether you like art or history, robots or weather, there is a museum for you!

Glossary

admission entrance fee for a place

ancient very old

archaeologists scientists who study the past by looking at objects

collections groups of similar things

curators people who choose and care for exhibits in a museum

emperors powerful rulers of empires

exhibit to show something in public

Learn More in the Library

Books

Hayes, Amy. *Discovering STEM at the Museum.* PowerKids Press, 2016.

Mattern, Joanne. *Historic Williamsburg: A Revolutionary City.* Red Chair Press, 2017.

Seeley, H.M. *America's Oddest Museums.* Gareth Stevens, 2017.

Verde, Susan. *The Museum.* Harry N. Abrams, 2013.

Index

About the Author

Joanne Mattern is the author of many nonfiction books for children. She enjoys writing about animals, history, and famous people and loves to bring science and history to life for young readers. Joanne lives in New York State with her husband, four children, and several pets and enjoys reading and music.